Helping Children See Jesus

ISBN: 978-1-64104-124-9

The Refuge
A Story of Martin Luther

Author: Hannah Pedrick
Illustrator/Computer Graphic Artist: Del Thompson

Victory!

Adapted from God's Prisoner of War:
Marjorie Isabel Harrison Jackson's Story
Used by permission of the Global Ministries
Team (Calvary Church, Lancaster, PA)
Adaptation: Tom Luttmann
Illustrator/Computer Graphic Artist: Del Thompson

When I Am Weak

Author: Kathryn E. Zappitella
Illustrator/Computer Graphic Artist: Del Thompson

© 2020 Bible Visuals International
PO Box 153, Akron, PA 17501
Phone: (717) 859-1131
www.biblevisuals.org

All rights reserved. No part of this publication may be reproduced, stored in a retrieval system or transmitted in any form by any means, electronic, mechanical, photocopy, recording or otherwise, without the prior permission of the publisher, except as provided by USA copyright law.

RELATED ITEMS

To access related items (such as activities, memory verse posters and translated texts) please visit our web store at shop.biblevisuals.org and enter 5760, 5770 or 5780 in the search box on the page.

FREE TEXT DOWNLOAD

To access a FREE printable copy of the teaching text (PDF format) in English or other available languages, enter S5760DL, S5770DL or S5780DL in the search box. Add the item to your cart, and use coupon code XTACSV17 at checkout. Once your order is processed you will receive an email with a link to the free download.

STUDENT ACTIVITES

These are included with the FREE printable copy of the English teaching text for this story. See the directions under Free Text Download (above) to access them.

TABLE OF CONTENTS

The Refuge	1-15
Victory!	16-30
When I Am Weak	31-45

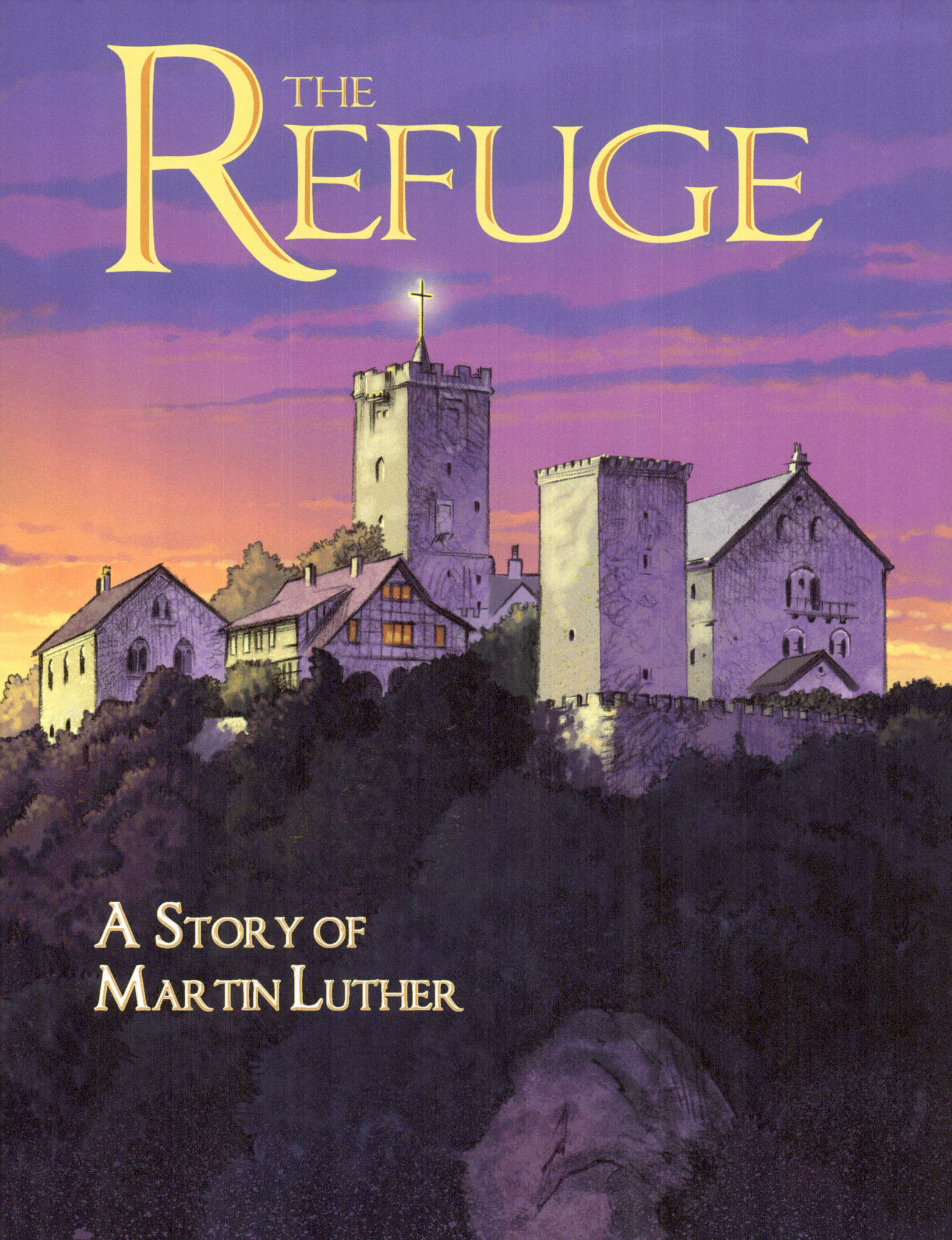

PRONOUNCIATION GUIDE:

Johannes	Yo-han-es	Wittenberg	Vit-ten-berg
Wartburg	Vart-berg	Worms	Verms

This story may be told in two, five or six sessions.

The circle (●) indicates where to divide the narrative when teaching two sessions.

The triangle (▶) indicates the breaks for five sessions.

The star (★) divides the narrative into six sessions.

Show Illustration #1

"I must find a place to hide!" Lightning lit up the sky as Martin Luther tried to hurry his horse to go faster through the slippery mud. The rain beat down on them, and thunder seemed to shake the air. Martin leaned toward his horse's neck and held on, trying to make himself as small as he could. And then, CRACK! A tree only a few feet away from him lit up with flames as lightning struck it. Martin's horse jumped in fear and Martin tumbled to the ground. There was nowhere to hide and nothing else he could do, so Martin cried out to God, "If you will save me from this storm, I will become a monk!"

 *Have you ever been afraid of a storm? Martin certainly was afraid of this storm, but he was even more fearful of the God who controls the weather. Martin knew that God is holy and perfect. He has no sin and He cannot have sin in His presence. God is also just. That means He promises to punish sin, and will keep His word as He always does. Martin knew he was a sinner and that he deserved this punishment that God promised. Do you know that's true for you and me too? You and I have broken God's law by our words, actions and thoughts, and we deserve punishment. In the book of Isaiah, God says, "And I will punish the world for their evil, and the wicked for their iniquity." (See Isaiah 13:11.) Martin hoped there was some way to escape this punishment and find a place of safety. He thought maybe he could find it by becoming a monk.*

Martin survived the storm and kept his promise to God. Nine days later he showed up in the town of Erfurt at the door of the monastery. (Show map.) This was supposed to be a place set apart from the rest of the world where Martin and the other monks could devote themselves completely to God, to prayer and to doing what was right. As Martin looked around at the peaceful gardens and the bell tower overhead, he thought, *Surely this is the place where I will find rest for my body and peace in my heart.*

★Show Illustration #2

Martin tried his best to be a good monk. He prayed long prayers and sometimes went without eating and drinking so he could think about God. He stayed awake for hours at night, and when he did sleep, it was often on a hard floor in a cold room. He went to the monks who were in charge of him and confessed to them any wrong thing he thought or did, trying not to leave anything out. He hoped that doing all these things would please God and save him from punishment, but he was still afraid it wasn't enough.

"If I could believe that God was not angry with me, I would stand on my head for joy," he said in frustration to one of his fellow monks.

Try as he did, Martin knew the terrible truth. He was still a sinner, still sinning and still facing punishment by God.

 Martin tried so hard, but he could never be perfect. Can you be perfect just by trying really hard? No. Only one person has ever been perfect. That person is Jesus, the only Son of God. Many years ago Jesus came to live here on earth. He never did one thing that was wrong, and He always did what was right. Jesus is the only person who was perfect. Even though he tried, Martin knew he was not perfect.

The monastery was not the place of safety Martin had hoped it would be, but maybe there was another place.

▶★ In the year 1510, Martin excitedly packed his few belongings–he was going to visit the Holy City of Rome. (Show map.) "Surely," Martin said to his friend as they started out, "I will find out how to get God to truly forgive me while I am in Rome."

"Yes," his friend answered. "After all, the Pope himself lives in Rome, and of all the leaders in our church, he is the one who is closest to God Himself."

NOTE TO THE TEACHER Gospel Points

 God's unconditional love	 Jesus' sacrificial death on the cross	Application for the believer
 Jesus is the only perfect Son of God	 Jesus has risen again!	
 All have sinned.	 Will you repent and accept Jesus as Saviour?	

Throughout the text of this story, we have included Gospel Point icons. These are suggestions to help you explain that gospel point to your class. These points are optional with the understanding that you may plan on presenting the gospel during your Bible time instead.

However, if this story is the only lesson being presented, please take advantage of this feature. Sow the gospel seed!

Show Illustration #3

When they reached Rome, Martin did everything he was supposed to do: he prayed, lit candles and gave money. On his hands and knees, Martin climbed the stone steps known as the *Scala Sancta*. These were supposed to be the same steps that Jesus had climbed right before he died on the cross. Martin stopped and prayed at each step, thinking that each one would, according to the church, earn some forgiveness from God. But when he reached the top, only one thought was going through his mind: *Who knows if this is really true?*

Martin was beginning to wonder what was true because of the church leaders he saw in Rome. Instead of finding them to be humble and sincere followers of God, he found that most were more concerned with feeding their bellies and building expensive church buildings. Some even told jokes in Latin while the common people, who didn't know the language, thought they were leading people in worshiping and praying to God.

Martin came back from Rome disappointed. Rome was not the place of holiness he had thought it would be: nothing he had done there had taken away his guilt of sin.

Soon Martin was traveling again, but this time to his new home in the town of Wittenberg. (Show map.) The leaders of the group of monks Martin was a part of sent him there to be a professor at the university. Martin was a good professor and he liked his work, but he was still worried about his sin. In fact, he thought about it so much that he began to be depressed and sick: sometimes he couldn't sleep. He knew he deserved punishment for his sin: nothing his church taught showed the way for him to be right with God.

After a few years of teaching other subjects, Martin was finally asked to teach the Bible instead. Martin was accustomed to hearing church leaders speak for God, but now he would be able to see what God said for Himself in His Word. As Martin studied the Bible, he began to notice things that were different from what his church had taught him. In the book of Romans he read: "The just shall live by faith." (See Romans 1:17.) Martin read the words over and over again: "The just shall live by faith." *Just*–that meant to be right with God. That's exactly what he was looking for. He had tried to become right with God by saying prayers, by confessing his sin, by doing lots of good things, by going to Rome and following all the rules; but the Bible said that a person who was "just" lived "by faith." Faith– that meant simply believing God, not trying to be good enough to earn anything from Him. And what had God done that Martin needed to believe?

Show Illustration #4

God had sent His own Son, Jesus, to die on the cross and give His precious blood to pay for all the wrong things Martin had done. Suddenly Martin realized that God had made a way for his sins to be forgiven. It wasn't through anything Martin could do; it was through what Jesus had done. All that was left was for Martin to believe this truth!

What Martin discovered in the Bible is true for you, too. Romans 6:23 reminds us that the "wages" or what we deserve for sin "is death" but Jesus, God's Son, died on the cross and gave His precious blood to take that punishment we deserve. Only He could do that because He is without sin. After Jesus died, He was buried; but three days later He rose from the dead because His payment for sin was accepted by God! Jesus is alive! That means that if you trust in Jesus and what he did to make things right between you and God, you will be forgiven of your sin. Romans 5:9 says, "Much more then, being now justified by his blood, we shall be saved from wrath through him." Believing in Jesus and turning from your sin is the only way to have your sins forgiven and be right with God.

After he had searched for so long, Martin discovered the refuge he'd been seeking. It was in Jesus! God had made it clear in His own Word, the Bible. Martin finally knew that God had forgiven him because of Jesus: he no longer needed to be afraid. This was good news, not just for Martin, but for everyone!

But it wasn't long before Martin realized that sharing the truth of the Bible was going to cause trouble.

●▶★ Trouble started when a man named Johannes Tetzel came to Wittenberg and began to sell indulgences. Indulgences were papers on which were written a promise from the Pope that God wouldn't punish you in a place called purgatory when you died. Tetzel told the people that if they bought this piece of paper, they could escape God's punishment. Selling indulgences was an easy way for the leaders of the church to make a lot of money.

Show Illustration #5

Martin knew that what Tetzel was saying was not in the Bible. So, Martin wrote what he called the "Ninety-five Theses," or 95 reasons why indulgences were wrong. According to his good friend, Philip Melanchton, on October 31, 1517, Martin posted it on the church door at Wittenberg for everyone to see and discuss. These Theses were quickly printed and translated into other languages for people all over Europe to read.

Martin's troubles soon got worse. The Pope, who was called Leo X, ordered that all of Martin's writings be burned and demanded that Martin take back what he had said. Martin was told he had to go to the city of Worms, in Germany, for a meeting (called the Diet of Worms) where the church leaders would decide what to do with him.

"Martin," one of his friends said, looking worried, "the leaders in Worms could order that you be killed because of what you believe."

"Or you could be captured by your enemies and killed even before you reached the city!" another friend reminded him.

Martin knew they were right, but he set out on the journey anyway. (Show map.) He rode with a friend in the back of an old wagon. Riding along with him were armed men who were supposed to protect him, but instead they found that in every town they came to, crowds of people ran out of their houses to cheer for him and throw flowers in his path. These common people believed the truth Martin taught from God's Word, even though the church leaders wanted to stop him.

When he arrived at Worms, Martin stood before the church leaders to answer their questions. "Are these your writings?" they asked.

"Yes," Martin answered.

"Will you recant?" they asked. "Will you take back everything you've written and said?"

Martin knew the importance of his answer. He asked for one day to decide.

★ Show Illustration #6

The next day, Martin was ready. "Unless I am convinced by the Bible or by clear reason (because I do not trust in the Pope or church leaders only, since everyone knows that they have often made mistakes and contradicted themselves), I must follow my conscience about what the Word of God says. I cannot and I will not retract anything, since it isn't safe or right to go against my conscience. Here I stand–I cannot do otherwise. May God help me."

▶ Even though he might have been afraid of what would happen, Martin knew that he was forever safe in Jesus. Even if he was killed, he would go to be in Heaven!

Martin was once so afraid of God. Now he knew that God loved him. Do you know that God loves you? He loves you more than any other person ever could. That's why He sent His Son Jesus to die for you. Martin finally understood this truth, and so he did not have to be afraid to die.

He would continue to trust God and declare the truth–no matter what.

The church leaders and princes debated Martin's fate for several days. Finally the decision was made. Martin was declared an outlaw. His writings were to be banned, and he was to be arrested. He could be killed by anyone who found him, and they wouldn't be punished. Furthermore, it would be a crime for anyone to help him or give him a place to hide. Martin had already left Worms before the decision was read, but he knew it was coming. He knew the trip home would be dangerous too.

Show Illustration #7

As Martin was traveling, his wagon was suddenly surrounded by horses ridden by men who carried crossbows.

★ They blindfolded Martin and forced him to ride with them. The men took him to a castle. "You are no longer Martin Luther the monk," they informed him. "You are Knight George, visitor to Wartburg Castle." One of Martin's most powerful friends had sent these men to kidnap Martin and bring him to a place where he would be safe. Martin stayed there in disguise for almost a year.

While Martin was in hiding, he wrote more than he had ever written before. His writings were copied and sent out for people to read. Martin also began another important project; he started to translate the Bible into the German language. In those days, the Bible was written in Latin, which only the important and educated people learned to read. Many of the regular German people had never read the Bible. They simply believed what was taught to them by the church leaders–the same leaders who were against Martin. Martin knew that in order for people to understand the truth of the Bible, they needed to be able to read it in their own language. And so he kept right on working.

▶ Martin continued to write and preach, trying to organize the new church that had started. There were many troubles along the way–sometimes Martin made mistakes; sometimes other people took what he had written and used them in the wrong way for things that were evil. Often Martin was disappointed when people didn't act the way he thought they should. There were times he was sad, angry and afraid. At times he wondered if God really loved him. But through it all, God helped Martin to remember that Jesus was his refuge. Martin wrote about this in a hymn for the church called "A Mighty Fortress Is Our God." (Sing hymn with students if able.)

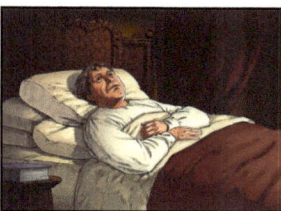

Show Illustration #8

When Martin was an old man and knew he was going to die, his friends heard him pray to God. He said, "I know as a certainty that I will live with You forever, and that no man shall be able to pluck me out of Your hands."

"Do you still believe everything that you taught about God's Word?" one of his friends asked quietly.

"Yes," Martin answered.

Martin had spent much of his life looking for a refuge–a shelter to hide in–and he had found it in Jesus. Whatever the danger, Jesus, through the truth of the Bible, was the answer to everything Martin Luther needed.

Jesus is the answer to everything you need, too. If you have never trusted Jesus to be your Saviour, the most important thing that you need is to have your sins forgiven, just as Martin did. The Bible tells you how that can happen. Acts 13:38-39 says ". . . that through this Man [Jesus] is preached unto you the forgiveness of sins: And by Him all that believe are justified from all things . . . ." Do you know that you have sinned and deserve to be punished for your sin? Do you believe that Jesus died on the cross and gave His precious blood to take the punishment for your sin, and then came alive again? Will you trust in Jesus as the only one who can save you? You can believe in Him today.

But maybe you have already believed in Jesus as your Saviour. Do you trust God's Word the way Martin Luther did? Decide to believe the Bible. Thank God that He has given you a Book that you can always trust to be the truth.

Review Questions

1. What scary thing happened to Martin Luther that made him decide to become a monk? *(He was almost killed in a storm.)*
2. What were some of the things Martin did to try to get God to forgive him? *(Prayed, didn't eat or drink, didn't sleep or slept on a hard floor, confessed)*
3. How did Martin feel about the city and the Church of Rome after he visited there? *(He was disappointed: it wasn't a holy place, and he still felt guilty.)*
4. What book did Martin finally begin to read to find out the truth? *(The Bible)*
5. Martin realized that he couldn't do enough good things to earn God's forgiveness. What was the one way that he could be forgiven? *(By believing in Jesus and trusting in what Jesus had done for him when He died on the cross)*
6. What did Martin do which first got him into trouble with church leaders? *(Wrote against some of the things the church was doing and teaching–the Ninety-Five Theses)*
7. When the church leaders called Martin to Worms and asked him to take back his writings, what did Martin say? *("I cannot and will not retract anything . . . here I stand–I cannot do otherwise.")*
8. On his way home, what did a friend of Martin's do to keep him safe? *(Kidnapped and took him to his castle to hide)*
9. While he was there in the castle, what important writing project did Martin work on? *(Translating the Bible into the German language)*
10. After all his troubles, did Martin still trust in God at the end of his life? *(Yes)*

Timeline

Directions: Use this to give background to the events in Martin Luther's life touched on in "The Refuge" story.

November 10, 1483: Martin was born in Saxony, a part of Germany) to Hans and Margarethe Luther. His father worked in the copper mines and did well enough to rise out of the peasant class.

1505: Luther earns his master's degree from the University of Erfurt.

1505: Luther enrolls in law school, then enters the monastery of the Hermits of St. Augustine at Erfurt.

1508: Luther arrives in Wittenberg to teach.

1510: Luther travels to Rome.

1512: Luther earns his doctorate and becomes a professor at the University of Wittenberg.

1515-16: Luther begins a serious study of the letters of Paul, particularly Romans and Galatians.

October 31, 1517: Luther posts the "Ninety-Five Theses" in Wittenberg.

1521: Luther is summoned to the town of Worms, Germany, for a diet, or meeting of the church. He is excommunicated. Luther spends ten months hiding in Wartburg Castle under the protection of Frederick the Wise, duke of Saxony, and begins translating the Bible into common German.

1522: Luther comes out of hiding and returns to Wittenberg. His translation of the German New Testament is published.

1525: Luther marries Katherine von Bora, a former nun.

By 1534: Luther and Katherine have six children, four of which survive.

1546: Luther dies.

God is our refuge and strength, a very present help in trouble. Psalm 46:1

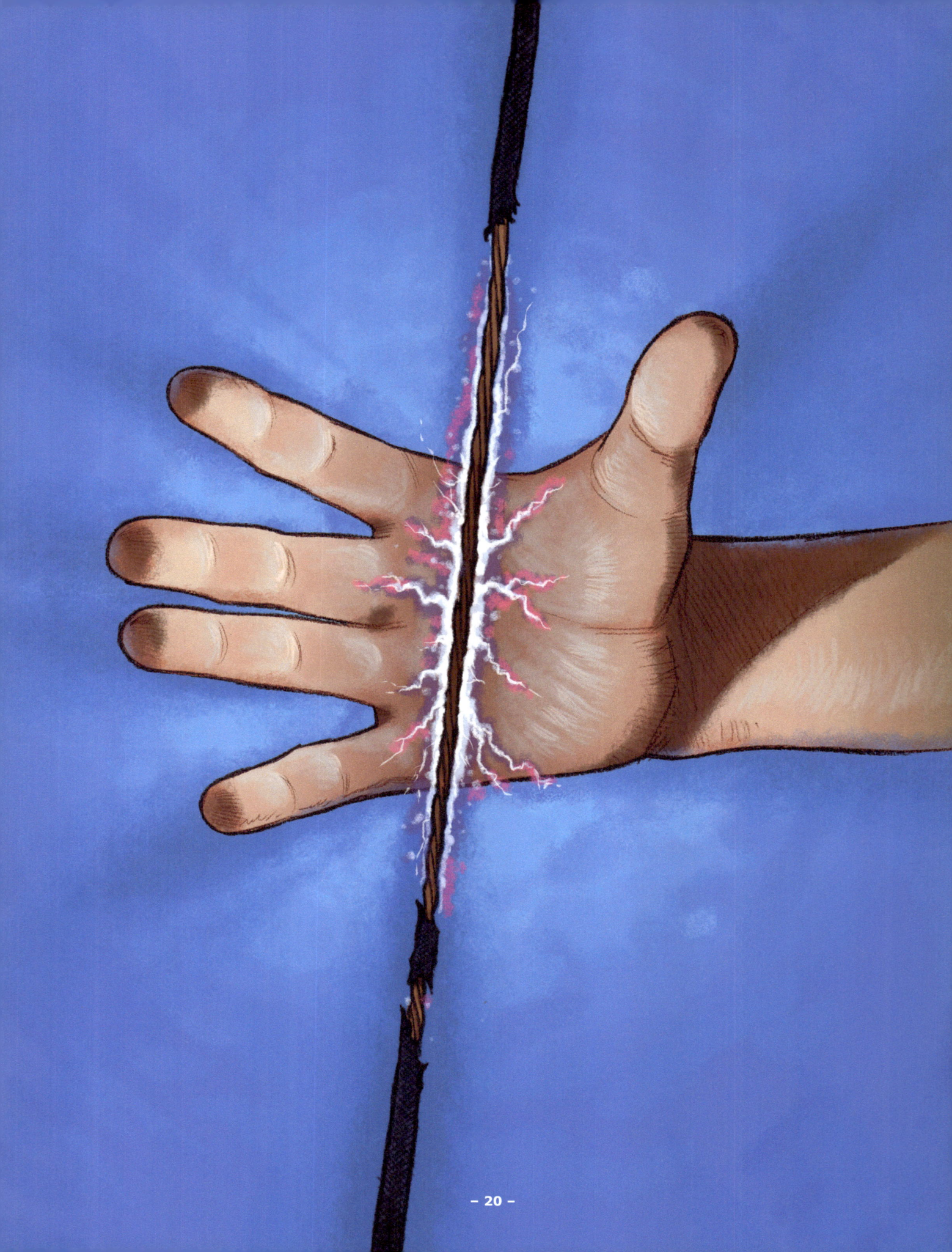

Beijing ★
Yantai (Chefoo)
Weifang
Weihsien POW Camp
Shanghai
Kunming

CHINA

Lesson Goal: To help children see the victory over sin and death found in Jesus Christ alone.

Memory Verse

But thanks be to God, which giveth us the victory through our Lord Jesus Christ. (1 Corinthians 15:57)

Show Illustration #15

"You are now our prisoners," the Japanese soldier shouted from the school courtyard.

"Tomorrow you will march to camp; tonight you pack one steamer trunk for each person."

Marjie was only ten but she knew what the Japanese soldier's words meant. She knew what the gun in his hands meant too. She and the rest of the students at the Chefoo Christian boarding school would not be free to leave.

It was 1942. Ever since the Japanese attack on Pearl Harbor the year before, there had been a danger the war would come to them. Now it had. How Marjie wished that her parents were there. Her father and mother were missionaries in China. That was where Marjie and her older brother Jim were, too, but China is a big country, and their parents were over 3,000 miles away from where the school was located. She had been away from them almost four years.

Marjie knew that even though she couldn't see her parents, her parents loved her. I want you to know that God loves you, too. You may not be able to see God, but He loves you very much and has shown His love to you in a special way. Keep listening.

Tears began to well up in Marjie's eyes, but she quickly brushed them away. She wanted to act brave for her brother.

"Come on," Jim whispered. "We have to get our things."

Under the careful watch of the Japanese soldiers, each packed their trunk. Little did they know that everything they put in them would have to last for the next three years!

Show Illustration #16

The next morning Marjie, Jim and the rest of the students and staff began their journey that would take them to Weihsien Prisoner of War Camp. Even though they were prisoners, someone began to sing as they marched, and soon everyone joined in. The words were from Psalm 46:

God is our refuge and strength,
in trouble a very present help.
Therefore we will not fear,
the Lord of Hosts is with us,
the God of Jacob is our refuge.

Don't you think those Japanese soldiers must have been surprised to hear the prisoners singing? These Christians knew that even though they were in the enemies' hands, God would help them. They knew that Jesus Christ had already defeated the enemy of sin and death by dying on the cross for our sins. We're reminded of that in 1 Corinthians 15:57 where it says, "But thanks be to God, which giveth us the victory through our Lord Jesus Christ." We are victorious in Christ!

As she sang, Marjie also remembered the words her mother had often repeated, "God will never leave you or forsake you."

Show Illustration #17

After the march, a stay in a temporary camp and a sea voyage, Marjie and the others finally arrived at the prison camp. Weihsien was surrounded by barbed wire and an eight-foot-high wall, with broken glass along the top of it. Armed guards were stationed around the wall and beyond it there was an electrified fence. There was no way of escape.

Just as there was no way to escape from the prison camp, there is no way we can escape the punishment for sin. Sin is anything we think, say or do that breaks God's law (give age appropriate examples). According to God's Own Word, you and I are sinners. Romans 3:23 says, "For all have sinned and come short of the glory of God." It's easy to see sin in others, but the truth is that we have all sinned and face certain punishment for that sin. Romans 2:3 says, "And thinkest thou this, O man, that judgest them which do such things, and doest the same, that thou shalt escape the judgment of God?" The answer is "no." You and I are guilty of sin, and there is nothing we can do ourselves to escape the punishment we deserve.

Marjie and over 1,800 other people from all over the world were soon packed into Weihsien. Every morning, the prisoners would have to report for roll call. The Japanese soldiers would shout, "Bang Go" ("number off") and each prisoner would have to reply when his or her turn came. Marjie's prisoner number

---

GOSPEL POINTS

- God's unconditional love
- Jesus is the only Perfect Son of God.
- All have sinned.
- Jesus' sacrificial death on the cross

- Jesus has risen again!
- Will you repent and accept Jesus as Saviour?
- Application for the believer

Throughout the text of this story, we have included Gospel Point icons. Beside these icons, there will be suggestions to help you explain that gospel point to your class. These points are optional with the understanding that you may plan on presenting the Gospel during your Bible lesson time instead.

However, if this story is the only lesson being presented, please take advantage of this feature. Sow the gospel seed!

was 133. Each morning she would pin onto her blouse a little cloth with this number. She had to wear it at all times.

All of the teachers from Marjie's school were prisoners as well, so despite conditions, classes were still held each day. Pencils and erasers soon wore down to stubs since there were no fresh supplies. Paper was used, erased, and used again until holes were worn through each sheet.

All of the children had chores. Jim had to pump water for the camp while Marjie had to learn to mend clothes.

I'm sure there were times that Jim and Marjie felt like disobeying and not doing their chores. The Bible tells us there is only one person who always did what was right all the time; that's Jesus Christ, the perfect Son of God! 1 Peter 2:22 says that Jesus "did no sin, neither was guile [deceit] found in his mouth." Jesus is God's Son and He is sinless.

To pass the rest of the time, Marjie and the other children made up games like catching and killing as many flies, bedbugs or rats as possible!

For food, the same meals were served every day. Bread porridge for breakfast and "S.O.S." or "Same Old Stew" for lunch and dinner. Eggs people snuck into the prison camp from outside were given to the sick for strength, but even the shells weren't thrown out. They were ground up into powder and fed to Marjie and the other children for calcium.

"Yuck!" exclaimed Marjie after gulping the powder. "I feel like I just ate a spoonful of sand."

While life at Weihsien was difficult, Marjie and the others soon got used to it, and one day seemed to pass the same as the next.

But Marjie never forgot one terrible day.

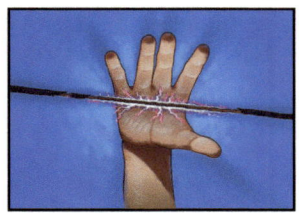
Show Illustration #18

During roll call one wet and rainy morning, one of the tall boys jumped up and grabbed a seldom-used electrical line that was hanging above the camp. He yelled, "Hey there's a current in this wire." Another boy named Brian called back, "You're kidding," but just as he reached up to grab the wire, the voltage became very strong. It knocked Brian down; there before their eyes, he was electrocuted.

Brian's death made Marjie and many of the children think about whether they were ready to meet the Lord if they were to die.

She remembered one night before the war when a special speaker had come to her school. The woman had shared the good news of the gospel that Jesus, God's Son, had come down to earth to die for the sins of everyone, including Marjie's.

While Marjie had heard the gospel before, she knew that she had never confessed her sin to God or trusted in Jesus to save her. That night after bed, she had tip-toed to her teacher, Miss Day's room. Instead of scolding her, Miss Day had taken the time to talk with Marjie about her need of Jesus, and Marjie had asked Jesus into her heart.

Did you know that Jesus came to die for you as well? The Bible says in Romans 5:8, "But God commendeth his love toward us, in that, while we were yet sinners, Christ died for us." That means that even though we are sinners deserving punishment, God still loves us and sent His Son to take the punishment for our sins. Only Jesus could do that because He is righteous and perfect like God the Father.

Jesus not only died for you, but He rose again victorious over sin and death! And the Bible says in Romans 10:9-10, "That if thou shalt confess with thy mouth the Lord Jesus, and shalt believe in thine heart that God hath raised him from the dead, thou shalt be saved." You can have freedom from the punishment and power of sin through Jesus Christ!

Now Marjie was in prison and had no bed other than the floor of her room, but that night she prayed, "Dear Lord, thank you for saving me from my sin and making a way for me to go to Heaven to be with you."

Marjie also thanked the Lord for giving her such a caring teacher as Miss Day. God provided the children with many caring teachers inside Weihsien prison camp, including one named Eric Liddell.

Show Illustration #19

"Uncle Eric," as he was known, was a missionary to China who had been imprisoned along with the others. Marjie heard that before coming to China, he had been a famous runner and had even won a gold medal in the 1924 Paris Olympic games. Now in the prison he continued to serve the Lord by helping and encouraging both young and old. Among the children he taught science classes and organized various games.

Our memory verse says, "But thanks be to God, which giveth us the victory through our Lord Jesus Christ." Eric's life was given to serving the Lord. He could do that whether in prison or not because Jesus had given him victory over the power of sin and serving self. If you know Christ as Saviour, you can have that same kind of victory over sin today, by continuing to place your faith and trust in Him.

Unknown to everyone else, Uncle Eric had been given the opportunity to be set free as part of a prisoner exchange with the British. However, he refused and gave his spot to a pregnant woman instead.

In the midst of helping everyone else, Uncle Eric became very sick. Because of his sacrifice he was unable to get proper medical treatment. One day Marjie and the other children received shocking news–Uncle Eric had died! The whole camp mourned for him but especially the boys who had lived in the same building with him. All the children sang at his funeral.

Marjie was sad too, but she was also happy knowing that Uncle Eric was no longer a prisoner. He was free and in Heaven with Jesus!

Show Illustration #20

One hot August day after almost three years of imprisonment, Marjie was lining up for roll call when someone shouted, "Look!" and pointed upward. There was an American B24 airplane flying overhead and dropping papers.

Marjie grabbed one as it settled on the ground. Her heart pounded with excitement as she read the words. It said for her and the others to remain calm. The Japanese would be surrendering, and American soldiers were coming to set them free! It ended with the words, "The end is near, do not be disheartened. We are thinking of you and making plans to rescue you."

She saw her brother Jim nearby. "Jim! Is it true? We're going to be free?"

Freedom! What would it be like to be free again? She wondered if her parents would even remember her. Between boarding school and imprisonment, almost seven years had passed since she had seen them!

Then she heard the sound of the airplane again. It made a second low pass over them and then turned again for another pass. On its third trip the bottom of the plane opened and 1, 2, 3, 4, 5, 6 and 7 multicolored red, turquoise, jade and peacock blue parachutes came puffing out! Marjie had never seen anything look so beautiful.

The US paratroopers landed just outside the gate.

"Come on, Marjie," Jim called. "Let's go meet them!"

Marjie, Jim and the others ran toward the front gate to meet the soldiers, but she wondered how the Japanese guards would respond? Would there be a firefight?

She soon knew the answer. Instead of forcing the prisoners back, the guards lowered their bayonets and let the people pass out of the main gate–out of the prison. The enemy had surrendered!

As the paratroopers landed they called out, "The war is over; America has won, and we have come to liberate you!"

 Do you know that is what Jesus came to do for you? Jesus, God's Son, came to this earth to give us freedom from the punishment and power of sin! Romans 8:1-2 says, "There is therefore now no condemnation to them which are in Christ Jesus, who walk not after the flesh, but after the Spirit. For the law of the Spirit of life in Christ Jesus hath made me free from the law of sin and death." Jesus Christ is our liberator!

Show Illustration #21

The crowd soon surged around the soldiers hugging and kissing them, shaking their hands and hoisting them up on their shoulders with a hero's welcome.

Some of the people laughed while others cried. After all the excitement of the day, Marjie went to bed that night thanking the Lord for their liberation.

While Marjie and her brother were no longer prisoners, they were still far from home and their parents.

They had to stay in China another month while regaining their health. They were very thin and undernourished. Before sailing across the Pacific onboard a US ship, they made a brief stop in a Chinese port. The mayor of the town welcomed them and gave each one a flyer that read, "Victory is won, peace is secured." They were also given a victory pin. Marjie fixed hers on the front of her dress where her prisoner number had been pinned.

After a month they arrived in San Francisco. Finally they boarded a train that would take them on the long trip to meet their parents who were now living in Toronto, Canada.

One night as they were traveling east, they stopped in a station in Calgary. Marjie's father met them there for the rest of the trip home. Marjie and Jim certainly looked older now, but as their father wrapped his arms around them, there was no doubt he still knew who they were.

Two days later they arrived in Toronto where their mother was waiting to meet them. When Marjie stepped off the train, there was a sea of faces in front of her, but she saw only her mother's face. They hugged and cried joyfully and gratefully. They were free. They were home.

Show Illustration #22

As she hugged Marjie, her mother looked down at her. "Did you remember God's promise?"

"Yes, Mom. He will never leave you or forsake you."

"That's right, dear. God always keeps his promises."

 *Do you remember the promise God has made to you in His Word? Romans 10:9-10 says, "That if thou shalt confess with thy mouth the Lord Jesus, and shalt believe in thine heart that God hath raised him from the dead, thou shalt be saved." Perhaps you are here today and you know that you have never asked Jesus, God's Son, to save you from your sins. You know that you have sinned and that there is nothing you can do yourself to escape sin's punishment and power. But you also believe that Jesus has died on the cross and risen again to give you freedom from your sin. If you believe that in your heart, you can confess it to God today and be set free!*

 *If you have trusted Christ, you can know for sure that you will never face the punishment for your sin. Christ has faced it for you, but you still need help every day to be victorious over the power of sin. Maybe you know of a sin in your heart that you keep doing again and again. Jesus can make you victorious over that sin. Confess it to him and ask Him for the help you need. You can be victorious!*

Epilogue

Since this is a true story, your students may naturally wonder what happened to Marjie after the war. Marjie and her family moved to Lancaster, Pennsylvania, in 1946.

The following year Marjie responded to God's call to be a missionary while attending a missions conference at Calvary Church. Her parents returned to China that same year to continue as missionaries there while Marjie and her siblings remained behind in the United States to finish their education.

Marjie attended college at the Philadelphia School of Bible where she met Walter Jackson. They were married in 1953 and went on to serve as missionaries to the Wayana people of Suriname.

After returning to the United States in 1971, Walter and Marjie served in Christian education in North Carolina. They then moved back to the Lancaster area where Walter became a pastor at Calvary Church. Marjie faithfully served along side her husband as a Bible teacher, pianist, childcare coordinator and missions conference organizer.

In 1999, Marjie was able to make a trip back to China to visit some of the people and places she remembered from her time there. She even made a brief visit to what was left of the Weihsien POW camp.

Marjie passed away on May 17th of 2012, resting in Christ and the blessed hope of eternal life. Her four children, twenty grandchildren and four great grandchildren all rise up and call her "Blessed." Many of them carry on her love and legacy to reach the lost here and around the world.

"O death, where is thy sting? O grave, where is thy victory? The sting of death is sin; and the strength of sin is the law. But thanks be to God, which giveth us the victory through our Lord Jesus Christ." (1 Corinthians 15:55-57)

REVIEW QUESTIONS

1. Where did Marjie and her brother Jim go to school? *(At the Chefoo Christian boarding school in China)*
2. Where were their parents? How far apart were they? What were they doing there? *(At another location in China that was 3,000 miles away, where they told Chinese people about Jesus)*
3. Who made the children leave their school? Why? *(Japanese soldiers. They were prisoners of the Japanese soldiers.)*
4. Where were the children made to walk? *(To a prisoner-of-war camp)*
5. What did some of the children and teachers do while they marched? *(They sang.)*
6. Name some things that describe the final camp they went to. *(Crowded; barbed wire; a high wall; electric fence; soldiers on guard)*
7. How long were they prisoners? *(Three years)*
8. What was life like for the children in the prisoner-of-war camp? *(They still had school. They made do with what they had or did without. Food was not great. The children did chores and played games.)*
9. The death of Brian and their teacher Eric helped the children with what important decision? *(The question of whether they were ready to meet Jesus if they died)*
10. About how many years passed since Marjie and Jim had seen their parents? *(Seven years)*
11. How were the children freed from prison? *(The war was over; planes and paratroopers rescued them.)*
12. What was the promise Marjie's mother was referring to when they met together after the war was over? *(God will never leave you or forsake you.)*

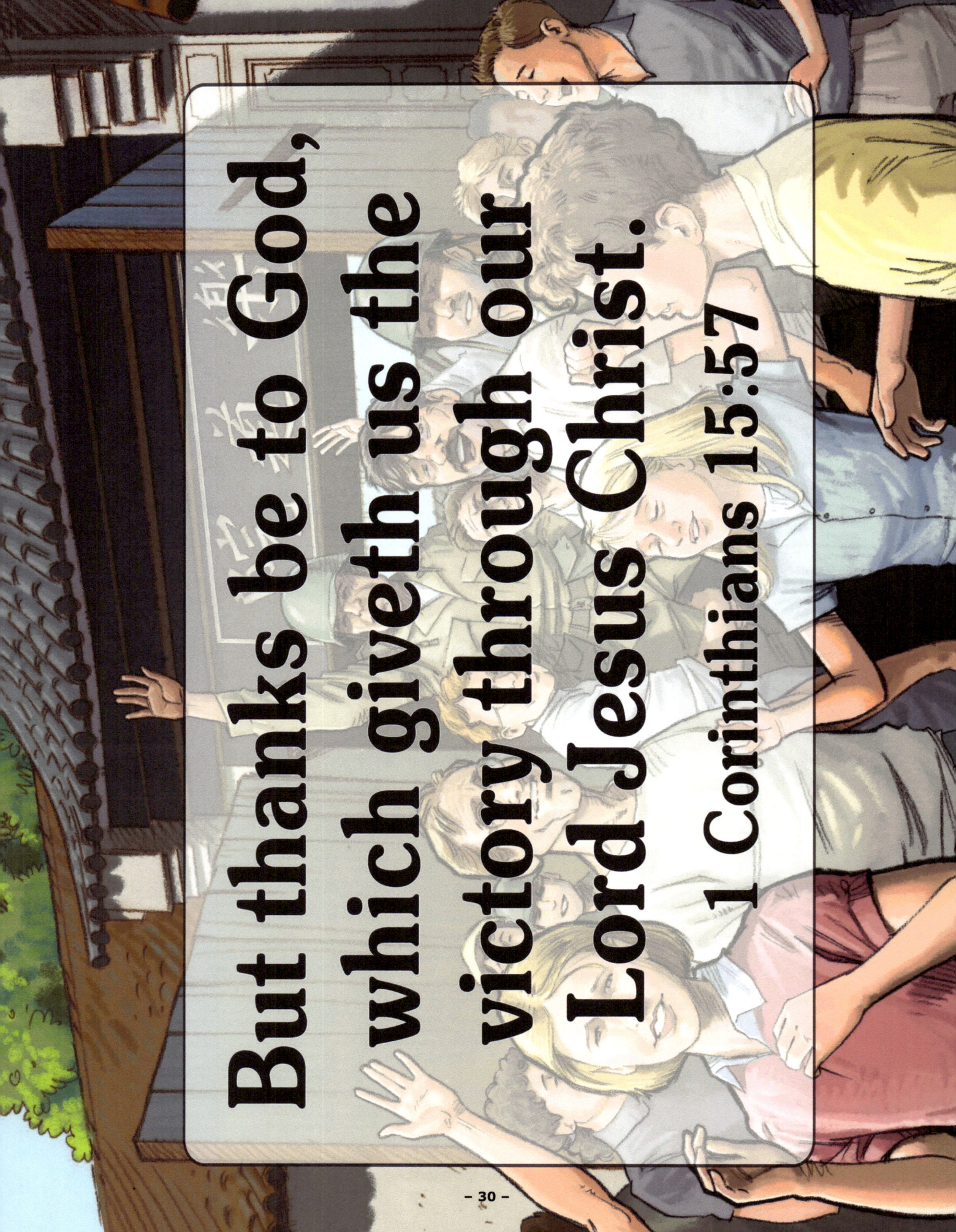

But thanks be to God, which giveth us the victory through our Lord Jesus Christ.
1 Corinthians 15:57

> **Note to the teacher**
> This story may be told in one or two sessions.
> The triangle (▶) indicates where to divide the narrative when teaching two sessions.

Show Illustration #29

On a bright, sunny Fourth of July, in the year 1791, the people of New Haven, Connecticut, were out in large crowds, excited to celebrate the 14th birthday of the United States of America. Rebecca Sherman peered out of her front door onto the bustling street, as she searched the crowds of happy holiday makers for her young grandson, Roger. Spotting him perched on the front fence, she called, "Roger! Time to come in for dinner!" The boy quickly jumped down from the fence and hurried inside where his grandfather was already seated at a large table. "Grandfather!" the boy exclaimed, "the people are speaking of you on the street! They look at the house as they go past and tell me that you are a great man and that our nation would not be as strong without you! What did you do, Grandfather? Did you defeat the whole British army? Are you a hero?"

Show Illustration #30

The elderly Roger Sherman took off his spectacles and smiled down at his young namesake. "No, no, I am certainly not a hero. The good people of this city have exaggerated the story a bit. I was trained as a shoemaker, not as a soldier. Besides, I was too old to fight in the war for our independence. Despite all this, God has blessed me by allowing me to help with the founding of our nation in such ways as I am able. But," he chuckled softly, "I have certainly done nothing to earn the name of 'hero,' unless you count the ability to make a good, strong shoe."

"Listen to the man!" exclaimed Rebecca, bringing a dish of meat to the table, which was now full with children, grandchildren, and friends. "Now, Roger dear, your grandfather may not have been a soldier, but he is being far too humble. Let me tell you a few stories, and you will soon see why people love and respect him. Now, hush!" She laughed, stopping her husband, who looked ready to protest. "You sit quietly and eat, my love, but I want to tell my family the story of a great and godly man, and of a great God."

Show Illustration #31

After Roger led a prayer of blessing for the meal, Rebecca continued her story. "Your grandfather was the second oldest in a family of seven children. After his father died, he had to leave school early to learn shoemaking and support his family. However, God had given him a passion for learning, and he was determined to learn all he could on his own. In fact, he would prop up books on his workbench and read in every spare moment he had! Even though he never finished school or went on to university, God blessed him as he taught himself. In fact, just recently Yale University gave him a college degree, saying he has learned enough to earn it even though he hasn't taken a single class!"

Show Illustration #30

The children around the table looked up eagerly, the younger Roger asking, "Do you think I could do that? I would be very happy not to go to school!" Down the table Uncle Josiah, Grandfather's younger brother, stopped midbite and chuckled. "Although you may not always love school, children, it is a good thing, I promise! I used to feel the same way about school, especially after our father died. I wanted to leave school and care for my family. But even though your grandfather was only 19 when our father died, he worked hard to provide for us. In fact, although he would have loved to go to university, he worked and saved so that my brothers and I could go."

Roger looked up at his grandfather. "Wasn't that hard, Grandfather? Giving up something you wanted so much and letting someone else do it?"

Roger Sherman put down his fork and looked around the table for a moment before speaking thoughtfully. "Yes, it was a difficult time in my life. Losing my father was very hard and so was becoming responsible for my family at such a young age. But it was during this time that I truly learned to depend on the Lord for my strength. It is easy to think that we are strong, and that we can do anything we want to if we work hard enough. But we really can't! Sometimes God brings us into hard times in order to show us how much we need Him. He loves us so very much and wants us to trust Him. During these years, God showed me my weaknesses and the greatness of Christ. I prayed that God would show me how I might serve Him–how to work hard, but also rely on Him, letting God lead me to do whatever He called me to do. God has richly answered that prayer!"

Rebecca passed around a plate of cookies, cut into stars like those on the first American flag, which she had helped her friend, Betsy Ross, sew (see map). She then picked up her story. "I would say so! With the strength of God, your grandfather moved on from being a shoemaker to being all kinds of other things: a surveyor (a man who measures the land using math); a lawyer; a justice of the peace; a member of the government of Connecticut and the government of the United States; even the mayor of New Haven!"

Uncle Josiah cut in, "Ah yes, your grandfather was known for his abilities with math. In fact, he used to write almanacs, books which forecast the weather and the seasons and good times to plant and harvest, all using math and the stars in the nightime sky! One day, after one of his almanacs had been published, Roger was in the town courtroom working as the justice of the peace. Another man jokingly reminded him that his almanac called for rain even though the skies were clear. The men around him thought it was a great joke, and they all went off to lunch laughing.

Show Illustration #32

But Roger was the only one to have a cloak that afternoon when, sure enough, it began to pour. That evening, your grandfather was the only man who came home dry!"

Amid the general laughter at this story, the elderly Roger smiled before adding, "Yes, God has blessed me in ways I never would have expected. But it wasn't always easy to trust Him. There were difficult times as well, especially when my dear first wife, Elizabeth, and two of our children died of illnesses. Through those dark times I struggled to remember that God loved me and that He was my strength. But," he remarked, looking at his wife with a twinkle in his eye, "little did I know the next blessing God had in store for me!"

Uncle Josiah grinned. "Roger came to visit me for a few days but was in a great hurry to leave and continue on to New Haven. I decided to ride with him for a short distance as he departed. While traveling down the road, who should appear riding toward us, but my wife's young niece, Rebecca, who was on her way to visit my wife.

Show Illustration #33

"Naturally, I stopped to greet her, expecting to spend just a moment before carrying on with our journey. However, much to my surprise, Roger no longer seemed in a hurry. As a matter of fact, he insisted on turning our horses around and accompanying Rebecca back to my home." Uncle Josiah looked around at the children with a mischievous smile. "And do you know how long your grandfather, who had been in such a hurry to leave his dear brother, stayed?" Giggling, the children shook their heads. "He stayed for several more days! I'm quite sure it wasn't my wife's cooking or my good conversation that kept him there either. Although Rebecca was 22 years younger than your grandfather, it didn't take long for them to discover that they wanted to stay together for much longer. They were soon married."

Grandfather laughed and remarked, "Your grandmother is quite the woman! I would be most helpless without her advice and care. And she is a beautiful woman, too!"

Show Illustration #34

"Did you know that one evening, when we were dining with many of our friends from Congress, George Washington himself escorted my wife into dinner, declaring that she was the prettiest lady in the room?"

Rebecca shook her head, half laughing, half vexed. "Oh, Roger, why do you tell the children such nonsense? Always remember, that handsome is as handsome does." "Well," replied her husband, "you looked handsome and acted handsome too, Rebecca; now it is my turn to praise you as a good example to our family." As the family enjoyed this story, playfully teasing Roger and Rebecca, young Roger took the opportunity to sneak another cookie or two from the plate before pulling his grandmother's sleeve. "But I still don't understand why the people in the street thought Grandfather was so important. How did he help our nation?"

▶"Goodness!" Rebecca replied. "I haven't even gotten to that part of the story, yet, and it is almost time to go to the town square for the Independence Day celebrations. Your grandfather was asked to help in the government very early, first here in Connecticut, and then with men from all the colonies. God has given him wisdom and thoughtfulness, and He put your grandfather in a place where he could use that wisdom to make good decisions for the colonies and eventually, for the United States of America.

Show Illustration #35

As a matter of fact, your grandfather is the only man who helped to write and also signed all four documents that formed our nation: the Continental Association, the Declaration of Independence, the Articles of Confederation and the Constitution! *And* he was the one who had the wisdom to come up with a solution when states were arguing about how the government should be set up."

"That's right," said Uncle Josiah. "The big states wanted representation by population and the small states wanted representation to be equal for all states."

"What did you do, Grandfather?" asked young Roger.

Sherman smiled. "Well . . . I compromised."

"That's right," Rebecca added with a nod. "He suggested a government with two parts–one represented by population and one represented equally. Some people called it the Connecticut Compromise or Sherman's Compromise, but the smart ones call it the Great Compromise because it helped solve a big problem and brought the states into agreement to form the nation."

"Well, now," interrupted her husband, "while it is true that I was asked to help quite often, I truly needed God's strength. I was not comfortable speaking in front of people. Many of the men in Congress had gone to a university and had been taught how to speak well. Who was I, a poor shoemaker? What could I say or do? But God helped me to proclaim what I believed was right, even when I wasn't comfortable doing it.

"Do you remember, children, what God said to the apostle Paul? He said, *My grace is sufficient for you, for My power is made perfect in weakness.*' That's why Paul could say, *Therefore I will boast all the more gladly of my weaknesses, so that the power of Christ may rest upon me.*

"God has helped me to keep those words in my heart. He's taught me to be thankful for my weaknesses, because through them the power of Christ is shown clearly! I especially need to remember that as I prepare to speak in public, as I must do this afternoon."

A murmur of laughter went around the table as Rebecca exclaimed, "Ah, yes, your grandfather does not always make the most impressive figure when he speaks.

Show Illustration #36

"He has always refused to wear a wig or dress in any finer clothing than the poor homemade things I sew. And he has such a way of standing, with one fist clenched at his side and the other clenched straight out before him! Although some men will laugh when they see him and hear the abrupt way in which he speaks, they soon stop when they hear what he has to say. Did you know," she added, looking around the table, "that Thomas Jefferson himself once said, 'That is Mr. Sherman of Connecticut, a man who never said a foolish thing in his life.'"

Uncle Josiah winked at his brother. "Well, I could probably give him an example or two!" The elderly Roger laughed. "I'm sure you could. Despite these words of praise, I know that I desperately need God each time I am given the responsibility of helping our nation. I am so easily tempted to trust in myself, or to seek to please people by saying and doing what they want me to. I have found great comfort and encouragement in reading God's Word. Every time I serve in Congress, I buy a new Bible to read and study during that session.

Show Illustration #37

"At the end of the session, I bring that Bible home and give it to one of you. I want you all to know how important it is to continue reading God's Word and growing more like Him. Although I am now over 70 years old, I still need God every hour, whether resting on His strength, fighting against pride or struggling with my temper."

"Speaking of your temper, that reminds me of one more story! Then we need to leave or you will be late for your speech," Rebecca exclaimed. "I remember one day when I clearly saw that God was working in your grandfather's life. Roger continued to care for his mother, even after he had a home and family of his own. Every morning, Roger would lead devotions with our family and any friends or students who happened to be staying with us. One of the children was very small at the time and kept interrupting your grandfather. Finally he reached down and gently tapped her, more as a warning to behave. However, his mother saw the action and immediately stood up, hobbled over to Roger, and slapped him right across the mouth, exclaiming, 'You slap your child, I slap mine!' I remember holding my breath, wondering how Roger would respond. I could see the anger flash in his eyes. But, after a pause, he gained control over his temper and calmly went on with the devotion, without referring to the incident at all. That was God helping him to honor his mother and to respond with humility.

"But now, we must hurry and get ready!"

Show Illustration #30

Rebecca jumped up from the table amid the laughter that resulted from this story and began directing the cleanup and the preparations to leave.

Roger turned to his grandson. "So," he concluded, resting his hand on the youngster's shoulder. "While I was involved in the founding of our nation, it was the hand of God that carried me through. Any gift I possess comes from Him. He helps me know what is true and right and gives me the courage to proclaim it. He alone deserves the glory and praise." The boy reached up and took his grandfather's hand. As they walked together out of the house, he responded thoughtfully, "Grandfather, I think I want to be like you when I grow up. I want to help our nation be strong and do what is right." Roger smiled. "I would love that, my son. But even more, I hope you grow up to love God and find your strength in Him, no matter where you serve Him."

Review Questions

1. What trade did Roger study as a young man? *(Shoemaking)*
2. Why did Roger have to leave school and help support his family? *(His father died when he was young.)*
3. How did Roger continue to learn, even though he had to leave school? *(He taught himself by reading while doing his work.)*
4. After his father died, who gave Roger strength for all he had to do? *(God)*
5. Name one of the jobs Roger was able to do. *(A surveyor, a lawyer, a justice of the peace, a member of the government of Connecticut and the government of the United States, the mayor of New Haven)*
6. What type of scientific books did Roger write? *(Almanacs)*
7. Who did Roger meet while visiting his brother, Josiah? *(Josiah's wife's niece, Rebecca, whom Roger later married)*
8. Who said Rebecca Sherman was the prettiest woman in the room? *(George Washington)*
9. Name one of the important documents Roger Sherman signed. *(The Continental Association, the Declaration of Independence, the Articles of Confederation and the Constitution)*
10. How did Roger help solve the problem of representation in government? *(He proposed a two-part system, one represented by population, one represented equally.)*
11. What was his solution called? *(The Great Compromise or The Connecticut Compromise or Sherman's Compromise)*
12. What are some weaknesses that God helped Roger overcome? *(His lack of education, his inability to speak well in public, his tendency to trust in himself or to please others, his temper)*
13. What did Roger look like when he spoke in public? *(No wig, homemade clothes, one fist clenched and the other clenched straight out in front of him)*
14. What book did Roger read while in Congress? *(The Bible)*
15. What did he do with the Bible after each session of Congress? *(He gave it to one of his children/grandchildren.)*
16. Who slapped Roger Sherman? *(His mother [Great-grandmother])*
17. Where does Roger say all our gifts and talents come from? *(God)*

And He said unto me, My grace is sufficient for thee: for My strength is made perfect in weakness. Most gladly therefore will I rather glory in my infirmities, that the power of Christ may rest upon me. . . . for when I am weak, then am I strong.

2 Corinthians 12: 9, 10b

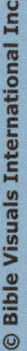

www.ingramcontent.com/pod-product-compliance
Lightning Source LLC
Chambersburg PA
CBHW041539220426
43663CB00002B/79